ELEPHANT SEALS

ELEPHANT SEALS

by Sylvia A. Johnson

Photographs by Frans Lanting

A Lerner Natural Science Book

Lerner Publications Company ▪ Minneapolis

Sylvia A. Johnson, Series Editor

The author wishes to thank Dr. Marianne Riedman, Monterey Bay Aquarium, Monterey, California, and Charles Deutsch, Department of Biology, University of California, Santa Cruz, for their assistance in the preparation of this book.

The photographer would like to thank the following people and organizations for their help with his work: Dr. Burney LeBoeuf and his co-workers at the University of California, Santa Cruz (Departments of Marine and Environmental Studies); Point Reyes Bird Observatory; United States Fish and Wildlife Service; Channel Islands National Park Service; National Marine Fisheries Service; California State Parks Department; Dr. Roger Luckenbach.

The glossary on page 46 gives definitions and pronunciations of words shown in **bold type** in the text.

LIBRARY OF CONGRESS CATALOGING-IN-PUBLICATION DATA

Johnson, Sylvia A.
   Elephant seals/by Sylvia A. Johnson; photographs by Frans Lanting.
      p. cm. — (A Lerner natural science book)
   Includes index.
   Summary: Describes the physical characteristics, habits, and natural environment of the elephant seals, so named because of their size and the proboscis that the males have on their noses.
    ISBN 0-8225-1487-7 (lib. bdg.)
   1. Northern elephant seal—Juvenile literature. [1. Northern elephant seal. 2. Seals (Animals)] I. Title. II. Series.
QL737/P64J63 1989   88-12924
599.74′8—dc19   CIP
                                          AC

Manufactured in the United States of America.

3 4 5 6 7 8 9 10 98 97 96 95 94 93 92 91 90

The shiny black eyes of the male elephant seal stare straight ahead. His proboscis dangles down in front of his mouth like a huge, baggy trunk. The seal is quiet now, but at any time he may throw his head back and produce a hollow, pulsing roar that can be heard all along the beach. He is the master of this beach, and this is his way of telling other males to keep away.

The beach is on Año Nuevo Island, near the coast of California. Every year in December, it is crowded with thousands of male and female elephant seals that have come out of the sea to mate and bear their young on land.

PINNIPEDS—THE FIN-FOOTED MAMMALS

The seals that come to Año Nuevo Island every year are northern elephant seals, among the largest of all seals. An adult male can reach 16 feet (about 5 meters) in length and weigh as much as two tons. Elephant seals were given their common name because of their great size and also because of the trunk-like **proboscis** on the heads of the males. The scientific name of the northern species is *Mirounga angustirostris*.

Elephant seals, like all their relatives, are mammals that spend much of their lives in or near the sea. Like other mammals, seals are warm-blooded and feed their young with milk produced by mammary glands. Instead of feet, a seal has four **flippers**, fin-like appendages used for swimming. The scientific name of the group to which seals belong—Pinnipedia—means "fin- (or feather-) footed" and refers to these versatile flippers.

There are about 33 different species of **pinnipeds** living in and around the world's oceans. They are divided into three large groups, or families. One family consists of walruses, those tusked giants of the Arctic Ocean. Another family is made up of both northern and southern elephant seals, as well as many smaller pinnipeds such as harbor and harp seals. Members of the third family include sleek sea lions, often seen in zoos and circuses, and fur seals, pinnipeds whose silky fur has often made them the target of hunters.

This photograph shows two representatives of the pinniped group. The large animals are northern elephant seals. In front of the seals and perched on top of their huge bodies are some California sea lions.

Opposite: Stormy seas surround the elephant seal colony on California's Año Nuevo Island.

BACK FROM EXTINCTION

Northern elephant seals have also been hunted, at one time so relentlessly that they almost became extinct. The big seals were sought not for their fur but for the six inches of **blubber,** or fat, under their skins. Blubber helps to keep seals and other sea mammals warm, but in the 1800s, people wanted it for making oil. Like whales, elephant seals were killed, and their blubber was stripped off and rendered into oil. Seal oil was burned in lamps and used for many other purposes.

By 1860, most of the elephant seals that lived along the coasts of California and Mexico had been killed. There were so few left that it was no longer practical to hunt them. By 1890, only one small group of seals, probably fewer than 100 animals, survived on Guadalupe Island, near Mexico's Baja Peninsula.

Since that time, however, the population of northern elephant seals has experienced a remarkable recovery. Because the animals are no longer hunted commercially, their numbers have gradually increased through reproduction. Laws passed by Mexico and the United States have also helped to protect the seals. Now there may be as many as 100,000 northern elephant seals, and their numbers are still growing.

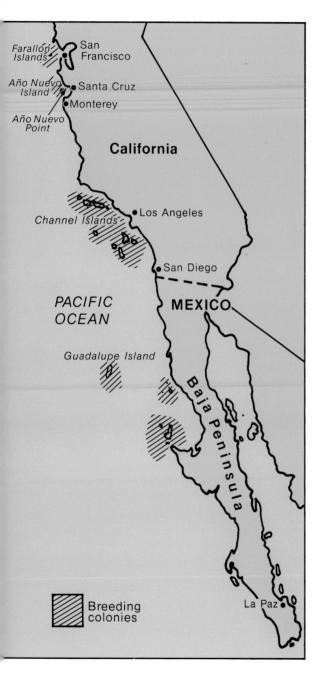

This map shows the areas where breeding colonies of northern elephant seals are located today.

Today, northern elephant seals can again be seen on islands scattered along the southern Pacific coast of North America. In 1955, they made their first appearance at California's Año Nuevo Island, and they have been coming back every year since then. When the colony on the island became too crowded, some seals began to go to nearby Año Nuevo Point, on the mainland. Since 1975, a breeding colony has existed here, not far from the city of Santa Cruz and only 60 miles down the coastal highway from San Francisco.

10

Northern elephant seals on the beach of Año Nuevo Island. One hundred years ago, these pinnipeds were almost extinct, but today their numbers are increasing.

"HAULING OUT"

The male elephant seals are the first to reach Año Nuevo early in December. They "haul out" onto the shore, moving awkwardly over the ground by balancing on their front flippers and humping their bodies like enormous caterpillars. (Unlike some of their relatives, elephant seals cannot "walk" on their flippers.)

An adult male elephant seal

Adult females are much smaller than the huge males.

Most of the adult male seals, or **bulls**, are making return trips to Año Nuevo. In fact, many of them were born here and have returned every year since their births. Not until a male is about eight years old, however, is he ready to take part in the yearly mating activities. At this age, he will be large and strong enough to fight for a place among the other male seals and for a chance to mate with the females.

The female seals, or **cows**, begin to arrive at the California coast in mid-December. They are also coming to find mates, but first they have a very important job to do: giving birth to their young.

About one week after she arrives at Año Nuevo, each female gives birth to a single seal **pup.** Elephant seal pups are born with their big eyes wide open and with coats of dark hair. They are small animals compared to the giant bulls, weighing about 70 to 100 pounds (32 to 45 kilograms) at birth. The pups will not stay small for long, however.

Nourished by its mother's rich milk, an elephant seal pup grows quickly.

Compared to some other young mammals, baby elephant seals grow quickly. In less than a month, they will weigh at least three times their birth weight and sometimes much more. (Most human babies are three months old before they even double their birth weight.) This rapid growth is due to a very nourishing diet: the female seals' rich milk. Seal milk, like the milk of other sea mammals, is high in fat and protein. Feeding only on its mother's milk, a seal pup can gain as much as 10 pounds (4.5 kilograms) each day.

These three pups are squeezed between
the large bodies of adult seals.

GROWING UP IN A SEAL COLONY

During the first month of its life, a pup spends most of its time nursing and sleeping. This might seem like a very peaceful existence, but the crowded beaches of Año Nuevo Island can be dangerous places for helpless baby seals.

One of the dangers that pups face is being injured by the adult seals. The big males are a serious threat to young seals, especially during mating activities. Bulls often run over and crush pups while they are chasing females or fighting other males. Adult females can also cause injuries by biting stray pups that are looking for food.

Another danger for pups is being lost in the crowd on the beach. Seal pups are completely dependent on their mothers for food and protection. If a cow and her pup become separated, the youngster will probably not survive. To prevent separation, a baby seal and its mother must be able to find each other amid the throng of other mothers and pups. One way that they do this is by making sounds.

Soon after a pup's birth, the cow begins to "sing" to her baby. She makes a high-pitched, warbling sound, and the pup responds with a kind of yapping. Through this duet, mother and baby learn to recognize each other's voices. If they are separated, they can keep calling until they are reunited.

Despite this system of communication, some seal pups do become permanently separated from their mothers during the first month of their lives. If these lost pups do not find another cow to feed and protect them, they are in a lot of trouble.

A female seal "singing" to her pup. The baby will learn to recognize its mother's voice and be able to find her on the crowded beach.

Some lost pups are lucky enough to be adopted by a cow whose own pup has been lost or killed. Then they will get the milk they need to grow and survive. Sometimes a cow is willing to nurse an orphan along with her own baby. Both pups may survive, but they will not be as fat and healthy as a pup with its own exclusive milk supply. Usually, females with babies will drive away or even attack a stray that is looking for a meal. Each year at Año Nuevo, many orphan pups die from injuries and lack of food.

While some pups are deprived of food, others manage to get a double share. These youngsters nurse from two females, their own mothers and another cow that doesn't mind (or notice) a guest at the dinner table. Sometimes they find a female to feed them after their own mothers have stopped nursing them. Such enterprising pups, who are often males, gain so much weight on this super diet that they look like overstuffed sausages.

This fat young seal is a "superweaner," a pup that got milk from another female after its own mother stopped nursing it.

PUPS ON THEIR OWN

After 27 days of nursing their pups, the female seals have completed their job as parents. Near the end of the nursing period, they mate with the male seals. After that, it is time for them to head back out to sea. During the month that the cows were on land, they did not eat at all. Now they are more than ready for a good meal of fish or squid.

Left behind by their mothers, the pups join together in small groups or **pods**. During this period of their lives, they are known as **weaners** because they have been weaned from their mothers' milk. The weaners still have a lot of developing to do, and they will stay on land for another two to three months. While they are there, they will not eat but will live on the fat stored in their plump bodies.

The weaners have already begun to lose their baby coats of black hair and to develop the smooth gray hair of adults. They have also started to teach themselves the skills of adult seals, entering the shallow water near the shore to practice swimming and diving. When they are not engaged in these activities, they play together or sleep in close-packed groups on the beach. By the middle of May, all the pups have left Año Nuevo for an independent life at sea. It will be several months before they haul their sleek bodies out on land again.

A group of weaners taking it easy on the beach

Right: A male pup whose proboscis is just starting to grow. *Below:* These young males are practicing the fighting skills they will need as adults. They are only playing now, but in the future, their fights will be in earnest.

A male and female elephant seal exchange vocal messages during the breeding season at Año Nuevo. While they are on land, the seals go without food, concentrating on the business of mating and bearing young.

THE MATING GAME

During the time that the female seals are nursing and watching over their pups, the bulls are busy with their own affairs. Male elephant seals play no part in raising the young. Their only contribution to the reproductive system is to mate with the females. Among elephant seals, however, this is not a simple job.

When female elephant seals come on shore at a breeding colony, they form groups that scientists call **harems.** A single male seal will try to get control of a harem and keep all the females in it for himself. His goal is to mate with the harem members while preventing other males from having the same opportunity. Since this goal is shared by all the male seals, the result is a complicated struggle for control.

The struggle begins as soon as the male elephant seals arrive at Año Nuevo in early December. The first males to haul out are usually the ones that controlled the harems during the last breeding season. Scientists call them **alpha males** because they are first in power and importance among the male seals. (Alpha is the first letter in the Greek alphabet.) Another name for one of these dominant males is **beachmaster**.

Beachmasters are usually large, powerful animals that are at least 10 years old. They have earned their top-ranking positions by fighting with other bulls, and they must continue to fight to stay in control. Each year, there are challengers that try to defeat the alpha males and take their places.

THREATS AND CHALLENGES

Conflict between two male seals usually starts with a threat rather than a fight. A male elephant seal can make a threat in several ways: by staring at another male, by moving toward him, or by producing a loud noise. The noise is made with the help of a bull's proboscis, the trunk-like structure on his head. During the breeding season, the proboscis serves as a kind of echo chamber for sounds produced in the seal's throat.

When a bull issues a vocal threat, he raises his upper body and throws back his head. With the end of his proboscis

Heads thrown back and mouths wide open, two male seals roar a challenge at each other.

The proboscis acts as an echo chamber for the sounds produced in a male seal's throat.

dangling into his open mouth, the seal produces a loud, pulsing sound that can be heard over a long distance. This sound says to other males, "I'm ready to take on all challengers."

If an alpha male is issuing the invitation, he often receives no reply. Weaker males recognize the voice of a beachmaster and keep their own mouths shut, afraid to challenge his authority. Only a few strong and confident bulls are willing to take on an alpha male in single combat. When one of these upstarts replies to a vocal threat, a battle is in the making.

The two seals move together, each continuing to issue loud threats. When they meet, the combatants stand chest to chest, their upper bodies held in a vertical position. Dodging and swaying like humans in a boxing ring, each seal tries to jab his sharp teeth into the opponent's neck and chest. This part of a male seal's body is protected by a shield of thickened skin, but the powerful blows still cause deep cuts that bleed heavily.

Exchanging vocal challenges, two male elephant seals move into position for battle.

Both seals are injured during the fierce encounter. They will continue to fight until one of them admits defeat.

Opposite: Surrounded by the members of his harem, a blood-stained alpha male warns other male seals to stay away.

Despite their fierceness, fights between male elephant seals almost never end in death for either animal. In many cases, the fight lasts less than a minute and is over when one seal gives up and backs away. In doing this, he is acknowledging the superiority of his rival. There will be no more battles between these two seals.

Sometimes a serious challenge to an alpha male results in an extended battle that ends up with both seals in the water. These fights often last as long as 45 minutes and stain the water for yards around with blood. An alpha male defeated in such a battle loses his top position and becomes inferior to his opponent and perhaps to other top-ranking bulls. The winner takes the loser's place as a beachmaster and gains control of a harem.

By means of threats and battles, the male seals at Año Nuevo eventually establish who is who in the social order. Each male knows which bulls are above him in rank and which ones are below. A bull knows that he will get into trouble if he tries to interfere with the activities of his superiors. On the other hand, he can push around any males below him in the social order.

A pair of elephant seals mating

WINNER TAKES ALL

The end result of this breeding system is that a very small number of male elephant seals mate with the females and become the fathers of next year's baby seals.

The alpha males, of course, do most of the mating within their harems. One beachmaster may mate with as many as 100 females in a single season. Bulls just under the alphas in rank usually hang around the edges of the harems. Sometimes they can avoid the beachmaster's watchful eye and sneak into the harem to mate with one of its members.

Most of the lower-ranking males at Año Nuevo spend their time in an area that some scientists call Losers' Beach. These bulls can't even get close to the females and have no opportunity to mate. Unless they can fight their way up the social order, the "losers" will die without producing any offspring.

Almost all the adult female seals, on the other hand, mate and have young every year. The pups that are born one year are the products of the previous year's mating. Elephant seal pups develop inside their mothers' bodies for eight months, but development does not begin until about three months after mating. This schedule makes it possible for the pups to be born at the same time each year, when the females haul out on land in December and January.

Two low-ranking males fighting at the end of the breeding season. Next year, these seals may have a chance to move up the social ladder and find mates.

This pup has just had its first encounter with the cold waters of the Pacific Ocean. Like all elephant seals, it will spend most of its life at sea.

LIFE AT SEA

By the end of March, all the adult male and female seals have left Año Nuevo. The mating activities are over for the year, and the seals are ready to resume their lives at sea. The pups will stay on land for another month, and then they will also take to the sea.

Scientists know quite a lot about how elephant seals live on land, but their activities at sea are not as well known. A researcher cannot follow a seal as it swims through the cold ocean waters or dives deep beneath the surface. We do have some information, however, about the seals' lives at sea, and we are gaining much more, thanks to the use of new scientific techniques.

Although elephant seals stay together on land, they seem to be loners when they are at sea. Scientists believe that each seal goes out on its own or perhaps in a small group to hunt the fish and squid that make up its food supply. When northern elephant seals leave their breeding grounds near the California and Mexican coasts, they seem to head north. The seals have been seen in waters off northern California, Oregon, Washington, and western Canada.

Slow and clumsy on land, elephant seals are quick and graceful in the water. They swim by stroking with their large hind flippers and by swinging the back parts of their flexible bodies from side to side. The front flippers are used mainly for steering.

An elephant seal's large hind flippers make it an excellent swimmer. This seal has a green identification tag attached to one of its flippers.

Diving is an important part of life at sea, and elephant seals are excellent divers, able to dive deep and to stay down a long time. Since all seals are air-breathing mammals, they have the same requirements as human divers who do not use special equipment. They must hold their breaths while they are submerged and must keep going without a fresh supply of oxygen. They must also avoid injuries caused by increased pressure underwater.

Like other sea mammals, elephant seals can stay underwater for a much longer time than any human diver. Females have been observed making dives that last as long as 45 minutes.

The length of an average dive is probably about 20 minutes. While the seals are underwater, they conserve their oxygen supply by slowing down most of their body systems. The oxygen in their blood is circulated to their brains and hearts but not to other body organs.

The muscles of elephant seals and other kinds of seals contain large quantities of oxygen stored in a red substance called **myoglobin**. This oxygen supply helps the animals to keep moving during a long dive. Seals have so much myoglobin that their muscles look very dark, almost black, in color.

For very deep dives, humans use submarines and other vehicles that shield them from the increased pressure at great depths. Elephant seals don't have this kind of protection, but their compact bodies are designed to withstand extreme pressure. When the seals are deep underwater, most of the air spaces in their lungs collapse so that they cannot be crushed by pressure. The air in their respiratory systems is contained only in the windpipe and other parts that are protected by hard cartilage.

How deep do northern elephant seals dive? Scientists have been able to measure some dives by attaching instruments to seals. Several animals were recorded as having gone to a depth of more than 3,300 feet (about 1,005 meters). Most dives are probably not so deep. The kind of fish that northern elephant seals eat are usually found at depths of 1,600 to 1,800 feet (487 to 548 meters). Many scientists believe that this is where the seals spend most of their time when diving.

Instruments that measure the depth of dives are helping scientists to learn more about the lives of elephant seals at sea. Other kinds of instruments will give us even more information. Some use tiny computers that can record a seal's heart rate and the speed at which it swims. New instruments being developed will measure temperature and other water conditions in areas where seals swim. With the information recorded by such devices, scientists will have a better idea of where seals go and what they do during the long months they spend at sea.

This young seal has fallen victim to one of the hazards of life at sea. Its neck is caught in a loop of plastic strapping. The "plastic pollution" of the world's oceans endangers elephant seals and many other sea animals.

Research on seals is conducted in the laboratory as well as in a natural environment. *Below:* A researcher at the Long Marine Laboratory of the University of California, Santa Cruz, takes notes on the behavior of a young elephant seal kept in a tank. *Right:* This captive seal has gotten hold of a fish too big to swallow.

A group of molting seals

THE YEARLY MOLT

After their breeding season ends, most northern elephant seals spend several months at sea, never even putting a flipper on the shore. Then they head back to land, this time not for breeding but for their annual **molt**.

Like all seals, elephant seals molt, or shed their fur, and grow a new coat every year. For some seals, molting is an easy process that takes place over several months. Elephant seals have a harder time. When they lose their fur, they also lose the outer layer of skin. During the process, their skins are exposed and sensitive. It takes about a month before the seals are again covered by a coat of sleek gray fur.

Northern elephant seals usually return to the place of their births for molting. The seals born in the Año Nuevo area haul out there to undergo the annual ordeal. They come on land at different times depending on their sex and age. From March to May, for example, adult females and young seals of both sexes haul out for molting. During the summer, adult males put in an appearance. After the seals have molted, they return to the sea.

While they are molting, elephant seals often flip sand onto their bodies to protect their sensitive skins from the sun.

ELEPHANT SEALS ON DISPLAY

When elephant seals began breeding on Año Nuevo Island in the 1960s, scientists were presented with a unique opportunity to study the large animals. By watching their activities over many seasons, researchers like Dr. Burney LeBoeuf of the University of California, Santa Cruz, learned a great deal about the way in which the seals found mates and raised their young.

In observing the elephant seals at Año Nuevo, scientists were faced with some problems. One of the most basic problems was how to recognize individual seals among the thousands on the island. In order to record and understand seal behavior, observers had to be able to tell one seal from another so they could know who was doing what when.

After trying several methods, scientists came up with a way of "writing" a name on a seal's back. They used a mixture of hair dye and bleach that lightened the animal's fur. With this liquid in a plastic squeeze bottle, a researcher would sneak up to a sleeping seal and write a name like Abe, Sonny, or Lucky on its back. (Fortunately, most of the animals were sound sleepers.) This label made it possible to identify the seal from a distance and to keep a record of its activities. Of course, it lasted only until the animal's next molt. For more permanent identification, scientists attached plastic tags to one of a seal's hind flippers.

The presence of elephant seals on Año Nuevo Island provided an important opportunity for scientific research. When the seals moved to the mainland in the 1970s, ordinary

These researchers are attaching an identification tag to a seal pup's flipper. The pup is not very pleased to be part of their research project.

people got a chance to observe these fascinating animals. All they had to do was get out of their cars and walk down to the beach in order to see the big seals fighting, mating, or feeding their young.

So many tourists came to Año Nuevo Point that problems soon began to develop. People were walking right up to the seals, staring and snapping photographs. The rangers in charge of the state reserve that includes Año Nuevo Point and Island were concerned about the safety of both seals and humans. What would happen, for example, if a male seal confused an upright human for a rival bull raising himself to make an attack?

A group of tourists observes a male elephant seal on the beach of Año Nuevo Point.

To avoid such problems, the number of visitors was restricted, and guided tours were established. Today, if you want to see the elephant seals of Año Nuevo Point, you have to make a reservation months in advance. Once pursued by hunters, elephant seals are now a popular tourist attraction. We can only hope that human curiosity will do them less harm than human greed did in the past.

GLOSSARY

alpha (AL-fuh) males—male animals that are at the top of the social order within a group. Alpha males dominate any other male members of the group.

beachmaster—an alpha male elephant seal that controls a harem and mates with its members

blubber—the layer of fat under the skin of seals and other sea mammals

bulls—male elephant seals

cows—female elephant seals

flippers—the paddle-like appendages of seals. A flipper is a kind of modified hand or foot. It contains five long bones, or digits, covered with a web of skin.

harems—the groups formed by female seals during the breeding season. One alpha male usually controls each harem.

molt—the shedding of fur or hair. Northern elephant seals molt and grow a new coat of fur each year.

myoglobin (MY-uh-glo-bihn)—a red pigment in the muscles of seals that stores oxygen

pinnipeds (PIN-ih-pehds)—animals that belong to the scientific order Pinnipedia. Seals, sea lions, and walruses are all members of this group.

pods—groups formed by young elephant seals that are independent from their mothers but not yet ready to go to sea

proboscis (pro-BAHS-ihs)—a long, flexible snout similar to an elephant's trunk

pups—baby elephant seals

weaners (WEEN-uhrs)—young seals that are no longer being nursed by their mothers

At California's Channel Islands National Park, elephant seals, sea lions, and plovers share a quiet beach at sunset.

INDEX